Christmas D

A beginner's guide to beadwork

Creative editor: Heather Kingsley-Heath
Managing editor: Sue Bartucca
Book design: Frank Bartucca
Printed by: Opal Print, Radstock

Other booklets in the series:
Daisy Chains, Beaded Mandalas, Earrings
Beading on a Loom, Peyote Designs

The Useful Booklet Company

The Useful Booklet Company is dedicated to bringing you beautiful beadwork designs with easy to follow, step-by-step instructions. All our designs can be adapted to suit your needs and we hope that our booklet will inspire you to create your own jewellery.

Contact us

For more information about *Christmas Decorations*, or other booklets in the series, please write to:

The Useful Booklet Company,
PO Box 3294, Stratton-on-the-Fosse,
Radstock BA3 4WL.
enquiries@usefulbooklet.com
www.usefulbooklet.com

Or turn to the mail order form on page 26

A guide to beads and equipment

Seed beads

Seed beads are small round beads that are graded in different sizes. In this booklet, we use size 11° seed beads because it is a nice size for beginners to work with. Seed beads come in two distinct types, round and cylinder, both of which are sold in a multitude of colours and finishes.

Round seed beads are round sided, whereas cylinder seed beads are flat sided and they have a larger hole through the centre. Several companies produce cylinder seed beads, but a common trade name is 'delica'. All the designs in *Christmas Decorations* use round seed beads but can be made from cylinder beads if you prefer. We list all the beads we use in each design in a shopping list at the beginning of each project, where one pack is equivalent to eight grammes of beads.

We also use assorted small glass beads and droplets in our designs, although these are optional in many cases. These beads are available from all good bead shops.

Bead quality

As you work it is important to discard any misshapen or chipped beads, because flawed beads can spoil the look of your work and a chipped bead has a sharp edge that could cut your thread.

Needles

It is essential to use the right needle for beadwork. Beading needles are thin and flexible so they can pass through the holes in beads without jamming. They also have a fairly long eye, which makes them easier to thread. Beading needles come in several different lengths and are sized from 10 to 15, where 10 is the thickest and 15 is the finest, we used a size 10 needle for all the *Christmas Decorations* projects.

Thread

Use strong, flexible thread that doesn't stretch and will tie into a tight knot that won't slip. The best threads to use for beading are multi filament nylon threads and there are several brands available. Two leading brands are 'Silamide' and 'Nymo'. We recommend a Nymo size D to start with. Use black thread when working with dark beads and pale grey or white thread when working with light coloured beads.

About the Christmas decorations

All our decorations can be adapted for any festive occasion, or just to decorate your home as light catchers in the window. Choose your favourite colours or ones to suit the occasion. To make your designs sparkle, use beads that are silver lined or ones that have bright, iridescent finishes.

Contents

Christmas trees

How to make a festive beaded tree

These hanging Christmas tree decorations are made using a simple beading technique called brick stitch.

> **Shopping list**
>
> 2 packs of size 11° seed beads:
> - 1 silver lined (SL) green
> - 1 silver lined (SL) red (optional)
>
> Assorted glass beads (optional)
>
> Beading needle, size 10
>
> Beading thread, size D, black

1 First you need to make a base row. To do this, thread your needle with a one metre length of thread, then pick up two SL green beads. Tie them together and pass the needle through one of the beads.

Pick up one more SL green bead, then pass the needle and thread back through the bead you started from. Pass the needle and thread back through the bead you just picked up and pull all the thread really tight. The beads should sit side by side, with the holes pointing top to bottom. Continue adding beads until you have completed a row of nine (a row of four are shown in our illustrations).

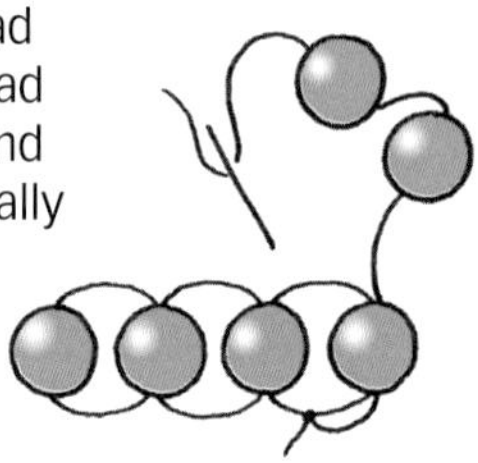

2 Bring the needle up through the last bead. Pick up two SL green beads and pass the needle under the loop of thread holding the bead next to the last one, and the one before it. Bring the needle and thread up through the second bead you picked up, down through the first one, then back up though the second one. This is how to start a row.

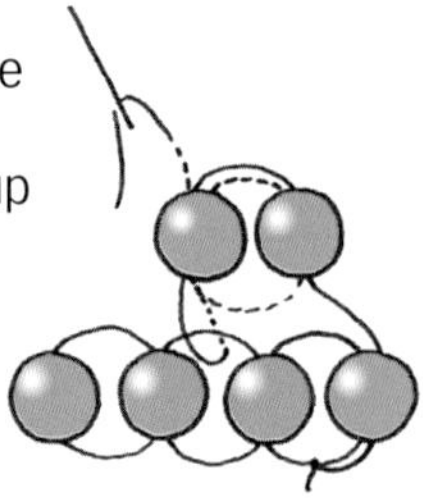

3 Pick up one SL green bead and pass the needle and thread under the next loop of thread holding the first row together, then back up through the bead. Pull the thread tight so that the beads sit closely together. Repeat this process to the end of the row, turn your work and start the next row with two beads.

Each row will be one bead less than the row before. Continue until you get to the two-bead row, then finish the thread by passing the needle back through the beads, knot it round an existing thread, then snip off the tail. Work in the tail from the beginning in the same way.

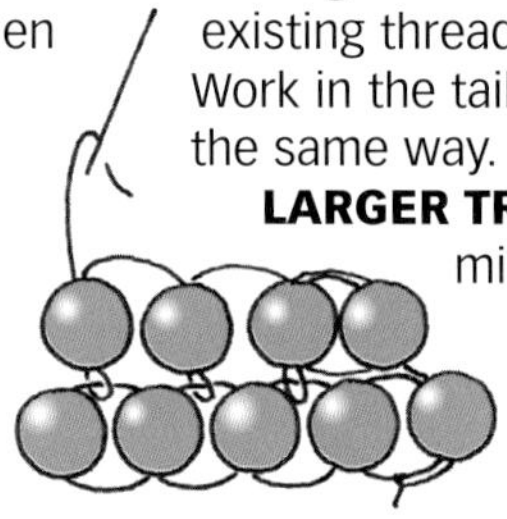

LARGER TRIANGLES: Start the middle triangle of the tree with a row of 13 beads and the bottom triangle with a row of 17 beads.

Our instructions are for the plain green tree on the left. Find out how to add red beads to your tree in the box below

How to make up the Christmas tree

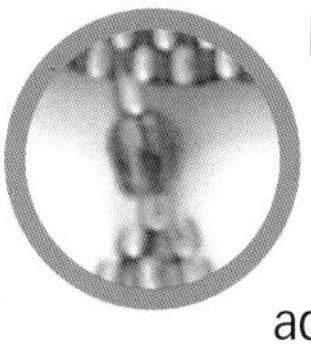

Using a new thread, start at the top of the smallest triangle and make a loop of 38 beads. Pass the needle down through the triangle, through the beads, and bring it out at the centre bead of the bottom row.

Pick up one SL green bead, one small glass bead and one SL green bead (or three seed beads). Pass the thread under the thread between the top two beads of the next triangle, back up through the three beads you just added, through some beads of the first triangle, then back down through to the second triangle, to the middle bead on the bottom row. Repeat this process to join the third triangle.

Decorate the bottom of the triangle with a tassel. Make a string of beads as long as you want, skip the last bead you added, then pass the needle up through all the other beads, knot the thread to the bottom row of the tree. Start the next fringe.

DECORATE THE EDGES: Add beads in a contrasting colour, such as red. Loop the thread with a bead on, under the thread of the bottom edge. To add beads to the side of your tree, pick up a SL red bead, pass through a few beads on the side of a triangle before picking up the next SL red bead.

Tinkerbell fairies

How to make a beaded fairy or angel

Tinkerbell's dress is made from a brick stitch triangle just like the ones on the Christmas tree (page 6), and the head and wings are made using a technique called circular peyote stitch.

Shopping list

2 packs of size 11° seed beads:
- 1 silver lined (SL) clear
- 1 silver lined (SL) gold

2 small glass beads

Beading needle, size 10

Beading thread, size D, white

1 Begin by making a brick stitch triangle with a start row of 14 SL clear beads (see page 6) and ending with a row of two beads. Then, with a new thread, bring the needle out between the end beads of the top and second row of the triangle. Pick up 13 SL clear beads and pass the needle through the end bead of the second-to-top row on the other side of the top of the triangle.

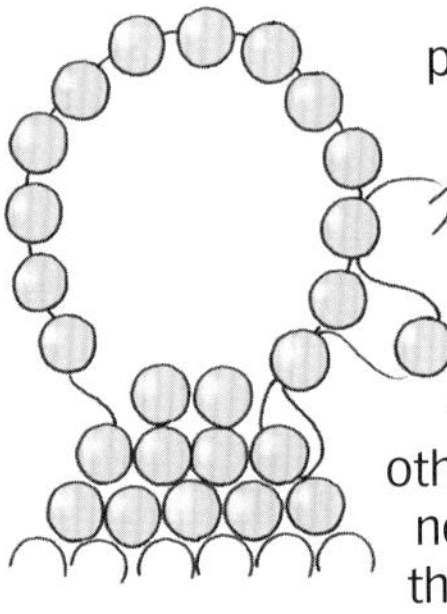

2 Pass the needle through the last bead of the loop you just added, then pick up one SL clear bead and pass the needle through the third bead on the loop, skipping the second one. Continue round the loop in this way, picking up a new SL clear bead, skipping a bead on the loop and passing through the next one. Pull the thread tight. When you get to the other end of Tinkerbell's head, pass the needle through the bead on the end of the second row of the triangle.

3 Pick up a bead, pass through the bead that is sticking up on the loop. Now pick up three SL gold beads and pass the needle through the next bead sticking up on the loop. Keep working round, adding in three SL gold beads in each gap. At the end of the row, pick up one SL clear bead, pass your needle through the end bead of the third row and finish off your thread.

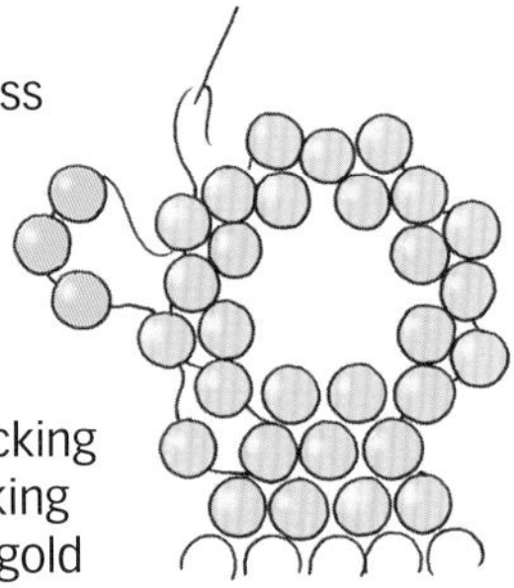

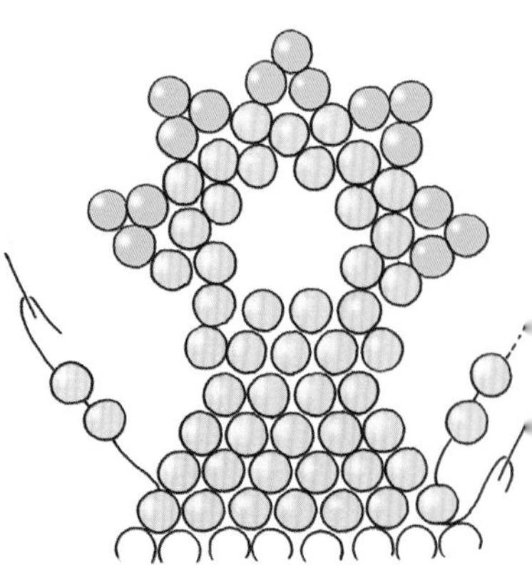

Add gold beads to your white Tinkerbell for a patterned border, or use the chart below to make a coloured dress

4 Tinkerbell wings are made in the same way as the head, but you start from the top of the end bead of the sixth row (from the top of the triangle). Pick up 43 SL clear beads, then pass the needle through the other end bead of the sixth row, passing from top to bottom of the bead. Pass the needle through the first bead of the loop, then work round as for the head. For the last row, just add one SL gold bead into each gap.

How to finish off

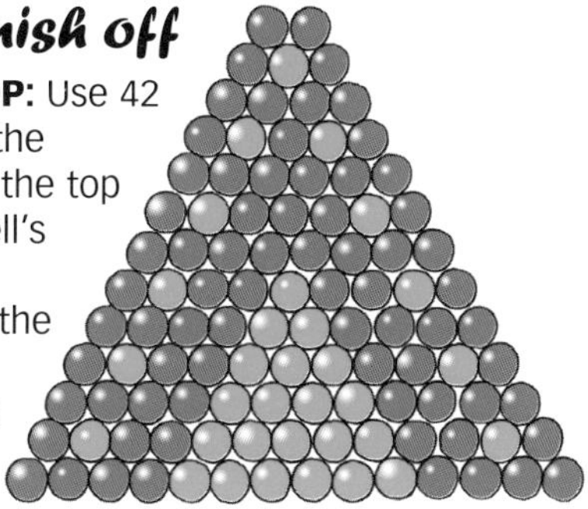

HANGING LOOP: Use 42 beads to make the hanging loop at the top of your Tinkerbell's wing loop.

LEGS: To make the legs, make two fringes from the centre of the triangle base, using a small glass bead for sparkly shoes.

ADDING A PATTERN: To add a pattern in your Tinkerbell's dress, follow our chart above for the blue design, or make up your own design using the blank brick stitch chart on page 25.

Midwinter snowflakes

How to make a snowflake

This snowflake design uses the circular peyote stitch you learned from the Tinkerbell fairies on page 8, and a technique called square stitch.

Shopping list

2 packs of size 11° seed beads:

- 1 silver lined (SL) turquoise
- 1 silver lined (SL) clear

Beading needle, size 10

Beading thread, size D, white

1 To start, make a ring of 12 SL turquoise beads and tie it into a tight knot. Pass the needle and thread through two of the beads in the ring. Pick up two more SL turquoise beads, pass the needle through the two beads on the ring again, then up through the first of the two beads you just added. Your new beads will sit above the beads on the ring with the holes pointing in a different direction as you work.

2 Pick up two SL turquoise beads, then pass your needle down through the second bead of the first pair you added, across to the first bead of that pair, then up through it and up through the first bead of the new pair. Keep working until you have seven pairs of beads sitting on top of each other. Pick up three SL turquoise beads. Pass the needle right through all the beads on one side, across the bottom, then through two beads on the ring. Start again to make the second point of the snowflake.

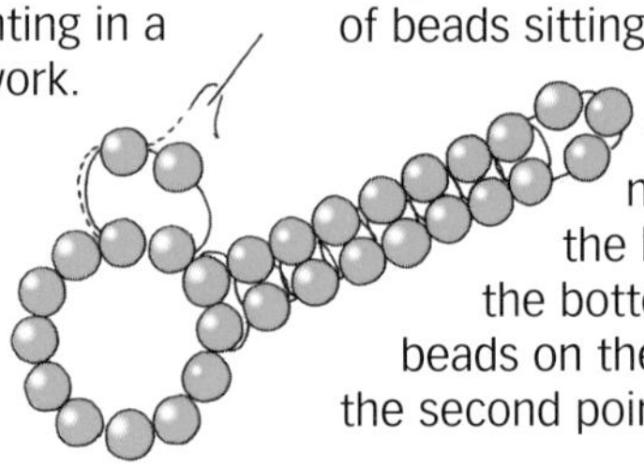

3 When you have six points on the ring, bring the needle up to the tip of the first point, and through the middle bead. Now change to circular peyote stitch. Pick up 11 SL clear beads and go though the middle bead of the next point over. Pick up 11 more and go across to the next point.

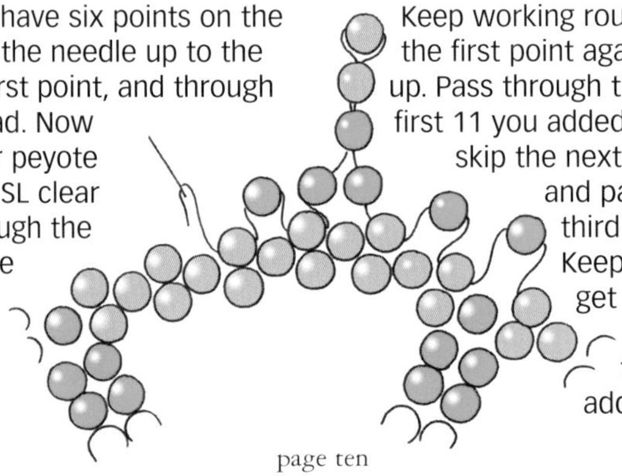

Keep working round until you get to the first point again. Pull the thread up. Pass through the first bead of the first 11 you added, pick up one bead, skip the next bead on the ring and pass through the third bead you added. Keep working, until you get to the beginning. Pass through the first bead you added for this row to

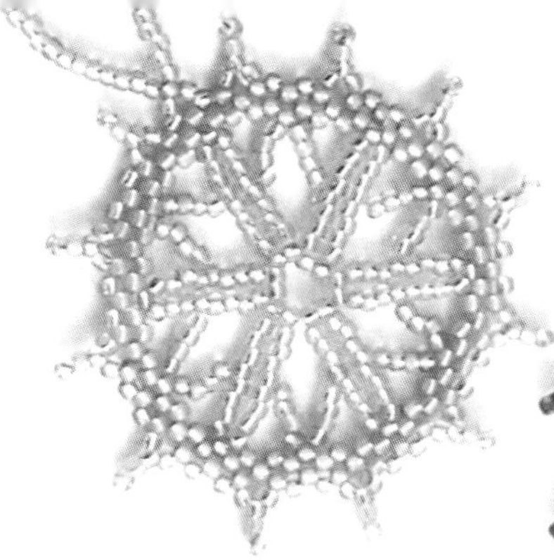

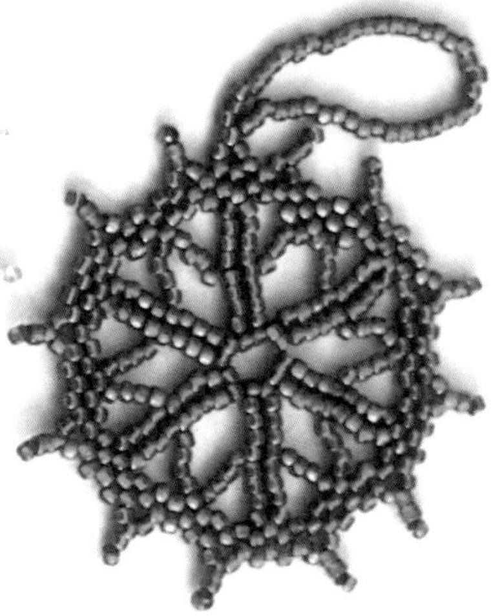

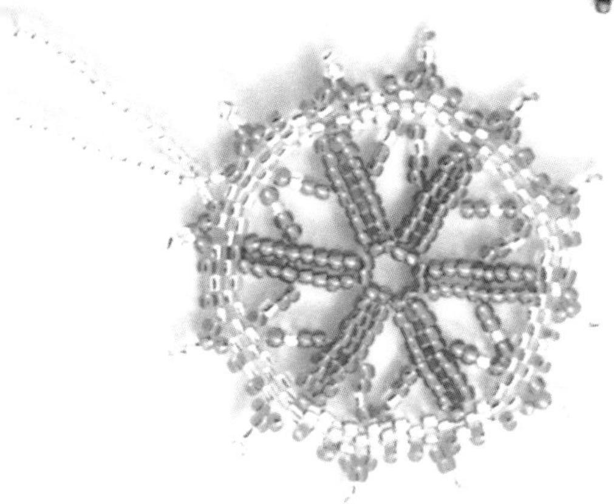

We have shown you how to make the blue and silver snowflake here, but as you can see from the photos, you can change the colours as you wish

4 To make the sides of the snowflake points, bring the needle out through to the inner edge of the ring. Come out through the centre bead, pick up one SL turquoise, one SL clear and two SL turquoise beads. Pass the needle down through the fifth bead from the tip of the spike, across the spike, up through the fifth bead on that side, then pick up two SL turquoise, one SL clear and one SL turquoise bead, and pass through the centre bead on the next section of the ring. Keep working round until each spike has two side bars.

Make a loop of 40 SL clear beads, positioned above the tip of one spike, to hang your snowflake from.

step up to the next row of the design.

The last row uses little points for sparkly snowflakes. Add one SL turquoise bead into the gap, through the next bead on the ring, then add two SL turquoise and two SL clear beads, skip the last SL clear bead, pass through the next SL clear and the next SL turquoise on the spike. Pick up one SL turquoise bead and go through the next bead on the ring. The row is made up of two single beads and one spike repeats (see illustration for step 3).

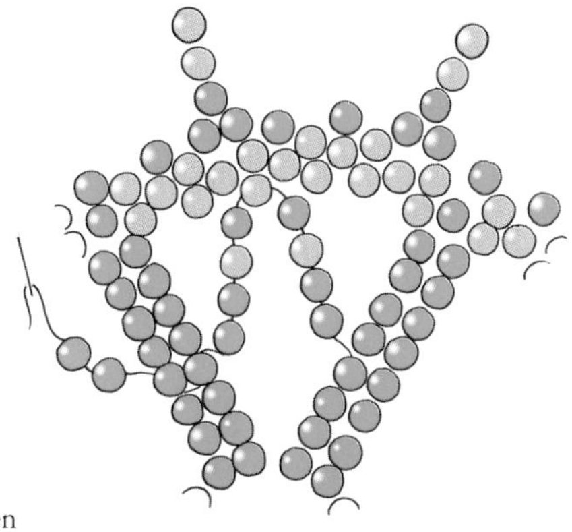

Festive jesters

How to make rings within rings

This design uses circular peyote just like the Tinkerbell design on page 6, but the first section starts a bit differently.

Shopping list

4 packs of size 11° seed beads:

- 1 matt red opaque
- 1 white opaque
- 1 silver lined (SL) gold
- 1 silver lined (SL) green

Beading needle, size 10

Beading thread, size D, black

1 To make the centre piece you work using a technique called flat round peyote. Just like circular peyote, but with a much smaller centre section. First make a ring of six red beads and tie it in a knot, pick up one more red bead then pass into the next bead on the ring. Continue round until you have six red beads sitting between the beads on the ring.

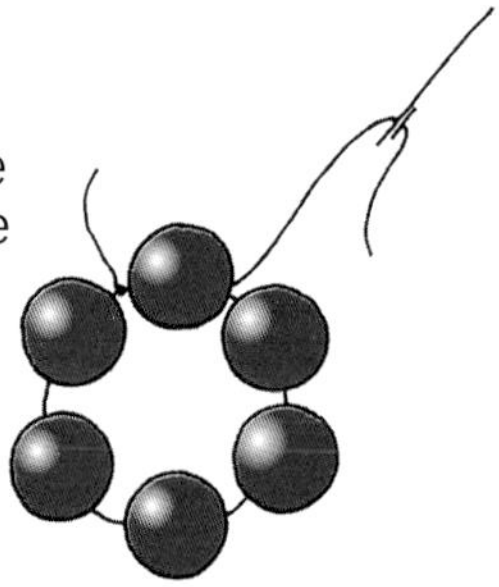

2 Pass the needle up through the first bead you added to step up to the next row. Pick up one red bead, pass through the red bead from the row before. Keep going round, then pass through the first bead of the row to step up. Pull your thread up tight so that the beads sit closely together.

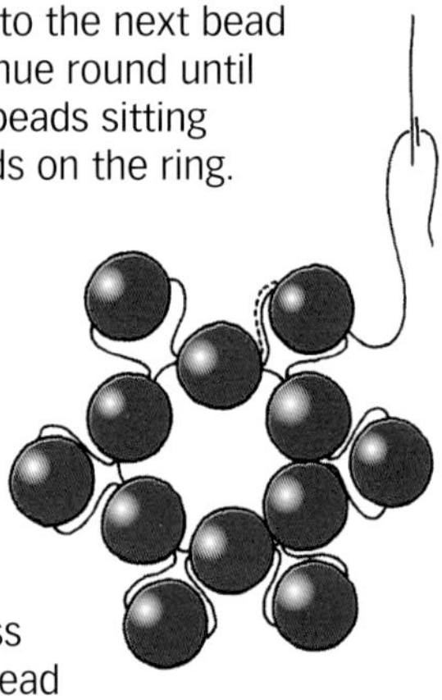

3 Pick up two white beads, then go though the red bead from the row before. Keep adding pairs of white beads between the red beads. Complete the ring with a row of gold beads, and finish off the thread.

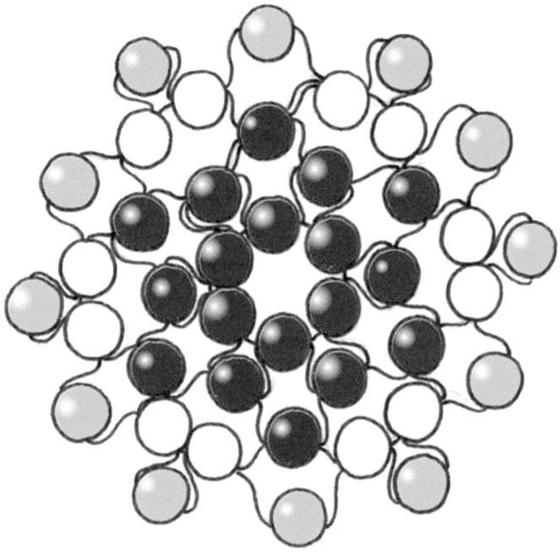

We use more flat round peyote ideas in our* Beaded Mandala *booklet, which is available to order on page 26. It contains nine different jewellery designs for you to try

For a different effect, try changing the bead colours to green, purple and gold, as in the design on the left in this photo

Adding the outer rings

The second and third rings are made in the same way as the Tinkerbell wings on page 6. Start by making a ring of 48 red beads and tie it in a tight knot. Pick up one white bead, skip one red bead on the ring and pass the needle into the next one to it. Add a white bead, skip a bead, continue round the ring, then pass up through the first white bead you added. The last row is worked by adding one SL gold bead into each space between the white beads.

To make the third ring, use the same technique but start with a ring of 74 white beads. Work a second row of red beads and a third row of SL gold beads.

How to finish off

To string your Festive jester rings together, start at the edge of the larger ring, make a loop of 48 beads, then pass the needle through the beads to the inner edge of the ring. Pick up two SL green beads, pass the needle and thread into the outer edge of the middle ring, through to the inner edge. Pick up two more SL green beads, pass the needle into the outer edge of the smallest ring, through to the opposite edge, then pick up another two SL green beads. Reverse the process until you reach the outer edge of the large ring. Finish off your thread.

Diamond drops

How to make a diamond hanging

This design uses brick stitch just like the Christmas trees (page 6) and Tinkerbells (page 8), but here we show you how to increase as well as decrease.

Shopping list

3 packs of size 11° seed beads:
- 1 silver lined (SL) green
- 1 silver lined (SL) silver
- 1 silver lined (SL) purple

2 frosted glass beads (optional)

6 size 8° frosted glass seed beads (optional)

Beading needle, size 10

Beading thread, size D, black

1 Tie two SL green beads together, bring the needle out through one of them and pick up two more SL green beads.

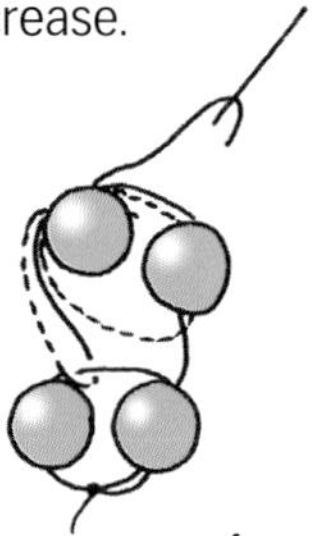

2 Pass the needle under the loop between the first two beads, then pass the needle up through the second bead you just added, down through the first bead, then across and up through the second bead. This is how you will start the increase rows.

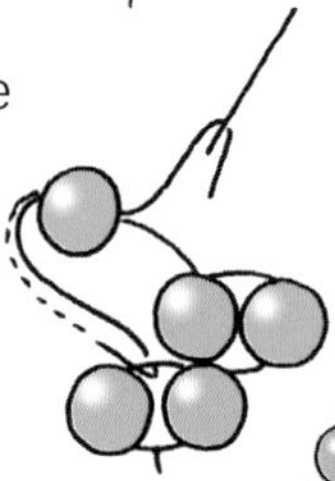

3 Pick up one SL green bead and pass the needle under the same loop, then back through the bead you just added. Start the third row. Add two beads into the first loop, then work across the row adding one bead at a time.

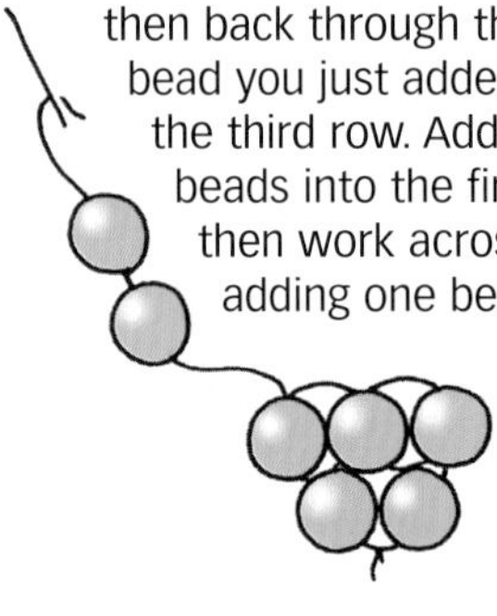

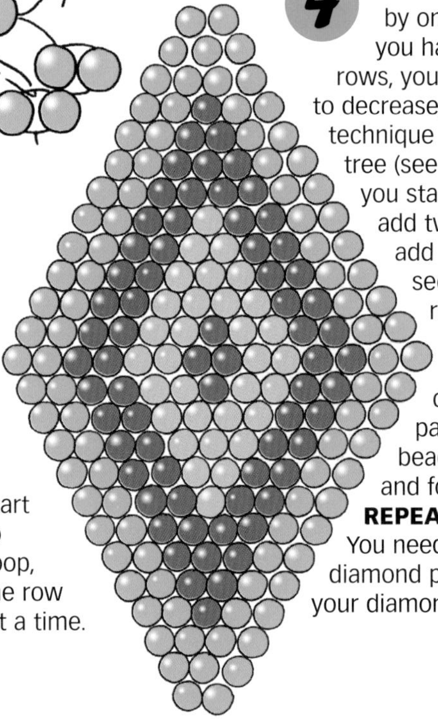

4 Each row will increase by one bead. When you have worked 13 rows, you need to change to decrease, using the same technique as the Christmas tree (see page 6). When you start a row you still add two beads, but add them into the second loop of the row before, not the first.

To add the coloured diamond pattern, count the beads as you work and follow this chart.

REPEAT FOUR TIMES: You need to make four diamond pieces to make up your diamond drop.

See the making up box below to find out how to finish the diamond drop and how to make the padded diamond drop (on the left in this picture)

How to make up your diamond drop

To complete your diamond drop, stitch two of the finished sections together along one side. To do this, pass the needle through two side beads of one section, then across to the second section and through two of the side beads. Keep working from one section to the other, lacing the edges together.

Now pick up the third section and lace it to one edge of one of the two you have already stitched. Finally, stitch the forth section to the two unstitched edges. The diamonds will curve inwards (see photo above).

LOOP: Make a loop of 48 beads, attach it to the top of the four diamonds, passing through a larger glass bead if you have one, then pass the needle down inside the decoration to the bottom. Add another glass bead, then make different length fringes using a mix of beads. Keep adding fringes until you are happy with the tassel, then finish off the thread.

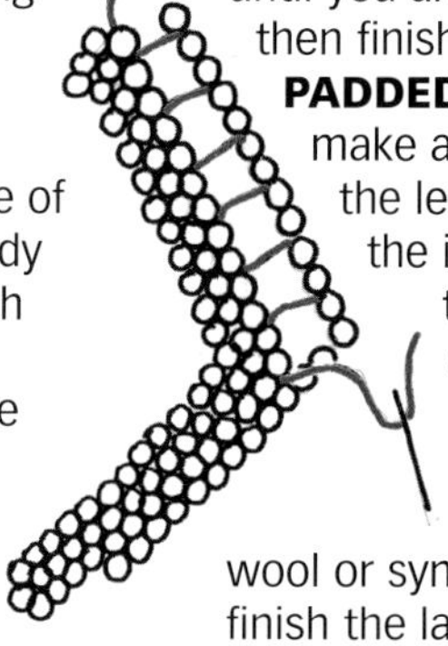

PADDED DIAMOND DROP: To make a padded diamond drop (on the left in the photo), follow all the instructions but just make three sections. Stitch these sections together, and before you stitch up the last seam, stuff the beadwork with cotton wool or synthetic toy stuffing, then finish the last seam.

Santa's parcels

How to make a present to hang on your tree

This parcel decoration uses 'two drop' square stitch which uses pairs of beads to make it quicker. The basics you need for the foundation rows of this technique can be found in the midwinter snowflake design on page 10, where you worked the first point of the snowflake.

Shopping list

2 packs of size 11° seed beads:
- 1 silver lined (SL) blue
- 1 silver lined (SL) bronze

Blue glass round and droplet beads (optional)

Beading needle, size 10

Beading thread, size D, black

Cotton wool or acrylic stuffing

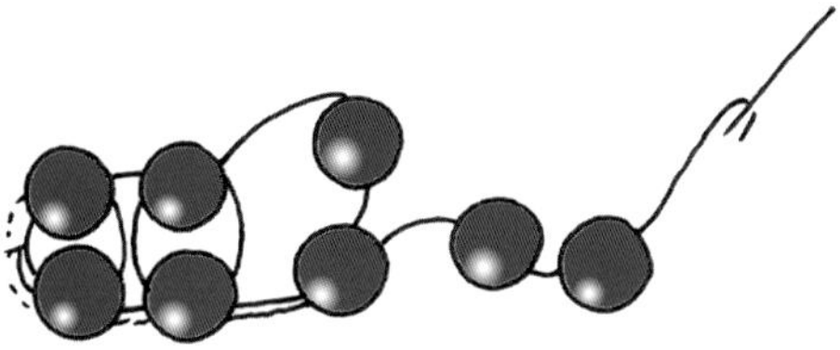

1 First tie two SL blue beads together, then bring the needle up through one of the beads. Pick up two more SL blue beads, and pass the needle down through one bead of the first pair and back up though the first bead of the second pair. Add another pair of SL blue beads, and keep looping back through the previous pairs until you have 11 pairs of beads sitting above each other.

As you work the beads will sit with the hole of each bead directly above the hole of the bead before.

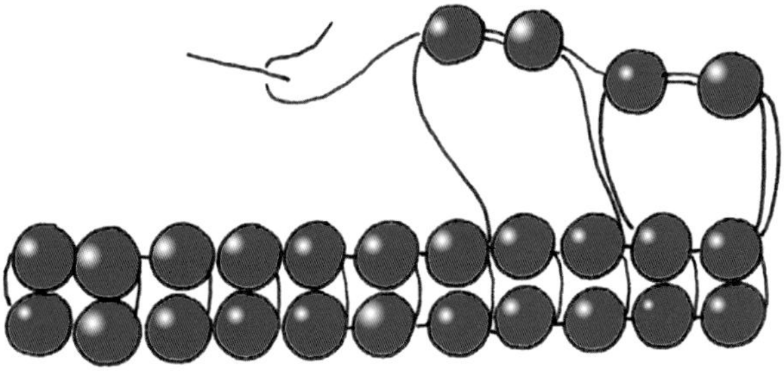

2 Pick up two SL blue beads, pass the needle back though two beads of the foundation row, then back through the two you just added. Then keep working along: pick up two SL blue beads, pass back through two beads and back through the two you added. Continue until the last bead, where you pick up just one bead, as each row has 11 beads. To make one square, work eight rows in total including the first two rows of the foundation.

TO MAKE A CUBE: You need to make three squares using SL blue beads and three squares using SL bronze beads.

For a different effect, try changing the bead colours for each side of your parcel, or add decorative beads to the fringes and vary the lengths of the strands

How to make up a Santa's parcel

To stitch the cube together, lay your squares so that a foundation row of one square lies beside the row ends of the next square. Stitch them together by passing through two beads of one square and under the loop at the row ends of the other one.

Stitch the squares into a cube with the three blue squares together and the three bronze squares together (see photo above). Before stitching the last seam, stuff the cube with cotton wool.

LOOP: Make a loop of beads and attach it to the corner where all three blue squares meet. Pass the needle down to the corner where all three bronze squares meet and make a tassel of fringes, adding decorative beads to the fringes if you wish.

Carnival baubles

How to make a beaded bauble cover

The Carnival bauble design uses the foundation row from brick stitch (see page 6) with a few extra beads added.

Shopping list

3 packs of size 11° seed beads:

- 1 colour lined (CL) violet
- 1 silver lined (SL) purple
- 1 silver lined (SL) green

12 glass faceted green beads (optional)

Beading needle, size 10

Beading thread, size D, black

1, 4cm diameter glass bauble, purple

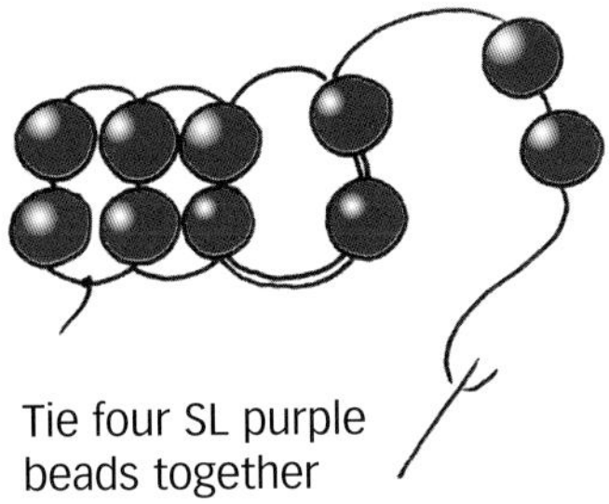

1 Tie four SL purple beads together and bring the needle through two of them. Pick up two more beads, pass the needle back though two beads, then back through the two beads you just added. Keep working until you have a foundation row of 18 pairs of SL purple beads, then join the first pair to the last pair to make a ring. Bring the needle out through one pair, pick up one SL purple, two CL violet, and one SL purple bead, count three pairs along on the ring and pass the needle through that pair.

Bring the needle back down and through the four beads you just added, then pick up four more in the same combination, back though the original four, and back through the new four. The beads will lie in the opposite direction to the beads on the ring.

2 Continue working until you have 14 sets of four beads in a row at right angles to the original ring. Pick up three SL purple beads, then work the needle and thread back through all the rows to the beginning. Pass the needle through the original ring then back out through the same bead you entered. Start the next set of four bead rows. Keep working until you have six sets of four bead rows hanging off the original ring.

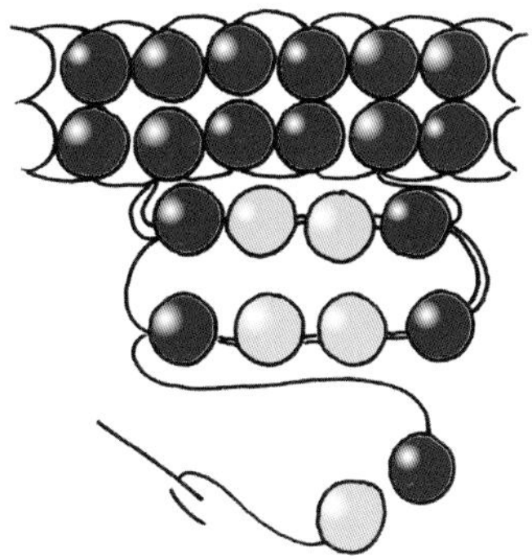

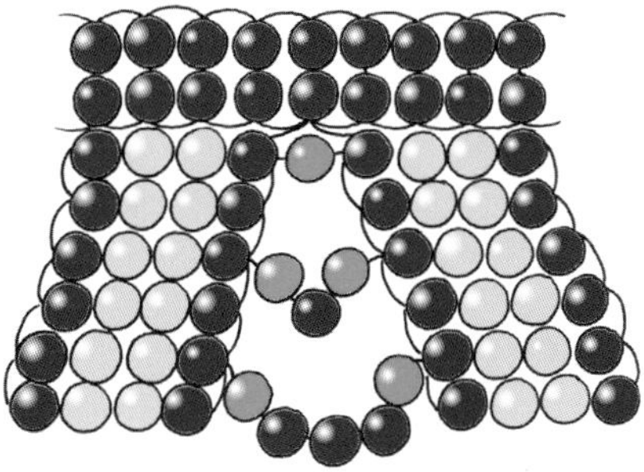

3 Add the rings. Bring the needle out through the first row (it helps to slide your original ring over the top of the bauble and work on the bauble, but don't squeeze). Pick up one green SL bead, then pass the needle through the first set of four of the next 'leg'. Keep working round until you reach the beginning. Pass the needle back through the next row of the first leg, and then out through the third row.

You are ready to start the next row, this time add, one SL green, one SL purple, and one SL green bead, then pass across into the third row of the next leg. End each row by passing through a row on the leg and coming out through the next one, so you skip a row each time.

Each ring section starts and ends with a SL green bead, and increases by two SL purple beads, as follows:

ROW 3: One SL green, three SL purple, and one SL green bead.

ROW 4: One SL green, five SL purple, and one SL green bead.

ROW 5: One SL green, seven SL purple, and one green bead.

ROW 6: One SL green, nine SL purple, one SL green bead.

ROW 7: One SL green, 11 SL purple, and one SL green bead.

Slip your Carnival beadwork over a purple glass bauble to add a stylish touch to your tree

How to make a fringe

The final touch is to add the drops. Work through row 11 to the centre of a row out through the fifth bead, add a fringe, then go in through the seventh bead. Pass the needle through the beads to the tip of the next leg, then add a fringe. Keep working round until each row and each leg tip has a fringe dangling from it, then finish off your thread.

Ballgown baubles

How to make a different style of bauble cover

This design starts in the same way as the Carnival bauble on page 18, but then uses circular netting instead.

Shopping list

2 packs of size 11° seed beads:
- 1 frosted turquoise
- 1 silver lined (SL) clear

1, 6cm diameter iridescent clear glass bauble

6 blue glass droplets (optional)

6 blue faceted glass beads (optional)

Beading needle, size 10

Beading thread, size D, white

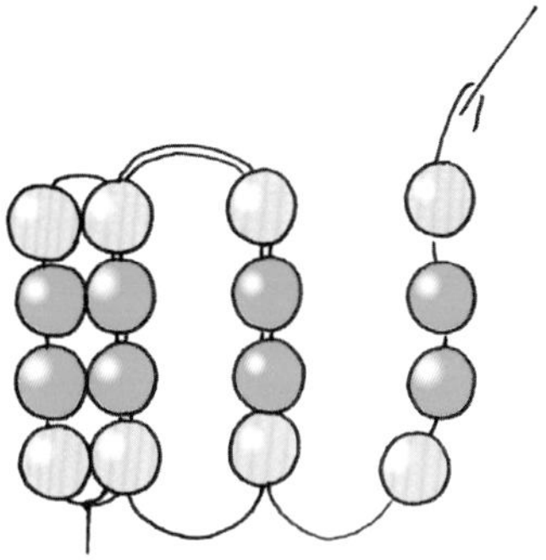

1 Make a ring using the steps on page 18, but this time work with four beads. Thread on one SL clear, two turquoise, two SL clear, two turquoise and one SL clear bead, and tie them together. Bring the needle out through one SL clear, two turquoise and one SL clear bead. Pick up one SL clear, two turquoise and one SL clear bead, and keep working in this sequence until you have a row of 18 sets of four beads. Join the first and last sets to form a ring.

2 **ROW 1:** Bring the needle out through a set, pick up two turquoise, one SL clear and two turquoise beads, then pass the needle through the fourth set of four beads on the original ring. Work through the beads and bring the needle out through the same hole you went into, then pick up two turquoise, one SL clear and two turquoise beads. Keep adding into the ring until you get back to the first set.

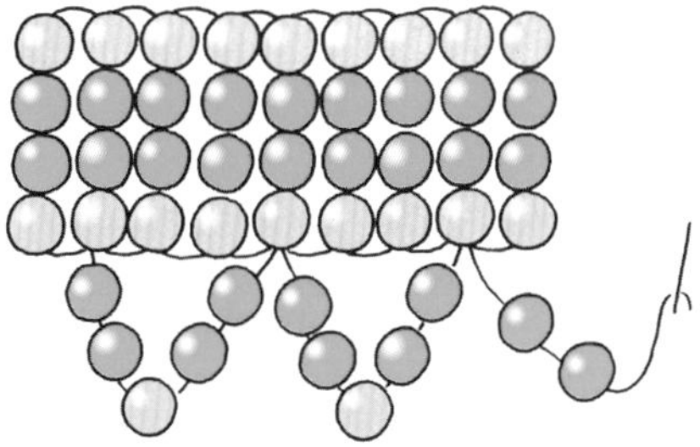

Top tip

Check that the ring will fit snugly over the top section of your chosen bauble. If it is too small, add three more sets of beads.

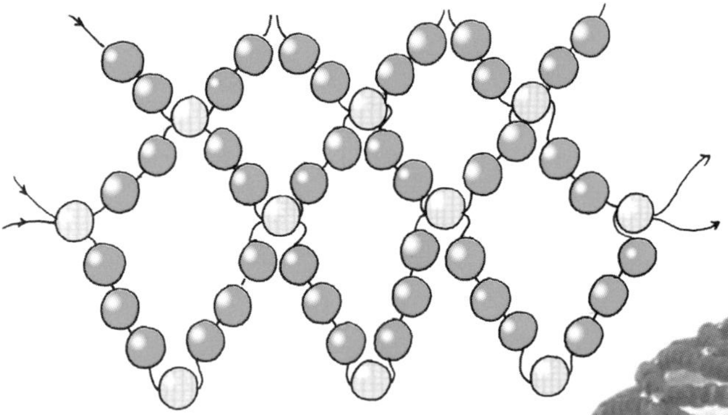

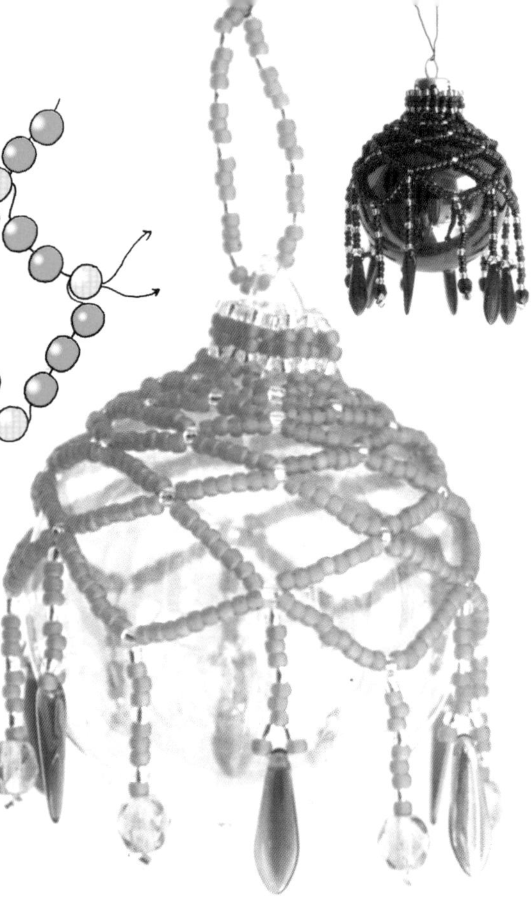

3 **ROW 2:** Bring the needle down through the first two turquoise and the SL clear bead of the first set you added. Pick up the same sequence, two turquoise, one SL clear, and two turquoise beads, and pass the needle through the SL clear bead of the next set over. Keep working round, adding the sequence and passing the needle through the SL clear bead. When you get back to the beginning, pass the needle through the first turquoise beads and the SL clear bead of the first set. Pull your thread up as you work.

Using different colours can completely change the look of your bauble cover. Decorative drop beads add that final touch

Top tip

You can add more beads to make a bigger bauble. Just add one bead either side of the SL clear bead.

4 To continue the rows increase the number of turquoise beads but always have a clear bead in the centre to pass through.
ROW 3: Three turquoise, one SL clear, and three turquoise beads. **ROW 4**: Four turquoise, one SL clear, and four turquoise beads. **ROW 5**: Five turquoise, one SL clear, and five turquoise beads. **ROW 6:** Six turquoise, one SL clear, and six turquoise beads. **ROW 7:** Seven turquoise, one SL clear, and seven turquoise beads. **ROW 8:** Eight turquoise, one SL clear, and eight turquoise beads. Finish off your thread.

Finally, add the fringes. Just as you did for the Carnival bauble (see page 18), work round the bottom row adding the fringes – add a fringe wherever there is a SL clear bead.

Square bunting

How to make bunting to decorate your tree

This design uses square stitch, just as you did for the Santa's parcel design (page 16) and daisy chains. It's easy to make and you can add all sorts of patterns to the basic design.

Shopping list

3 packs of size 11° seed beads:
- 1 matt red opaque
- 1 white opaque
- 1 green opaque

Beading needle, size 10

Beading thread, size D, black

1 Start by making a ring of 24 beads and tie it into a loop. This will be the loop to hang one end of your bunting with. Add two green, four red and one white seed bead. Pass the needle back down through the first red bead, pick up two more red beads and pass the needle back up through the last red bead before the white bead. Pick up two green beads.

This is the daisy chain section which sits between each piece of the square bunting.

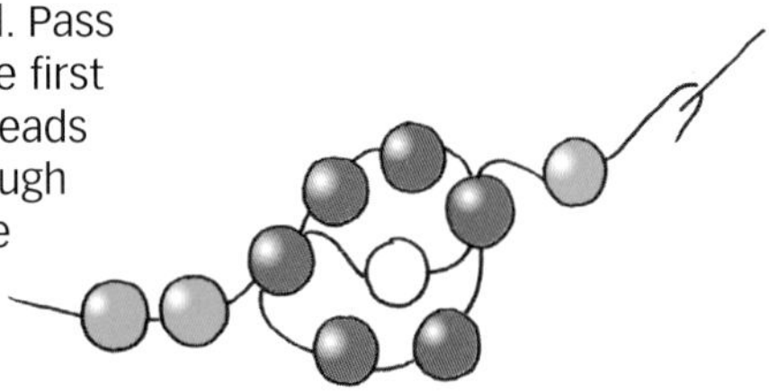

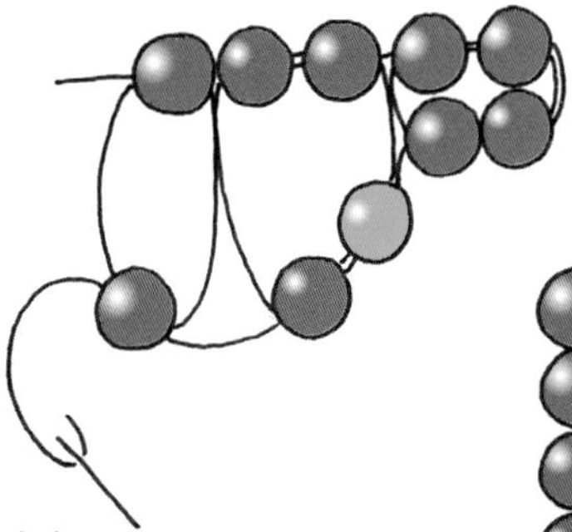

2 Pick up five red beads, then pick up two red beads, pass the needle and thread back through beads four and five, then back through the beads you just added. Pick up one green and one red bead, then go back through beads two and three and the beads you just added. Now pick up one red bead, and go back through bead five and the single bead you just added.

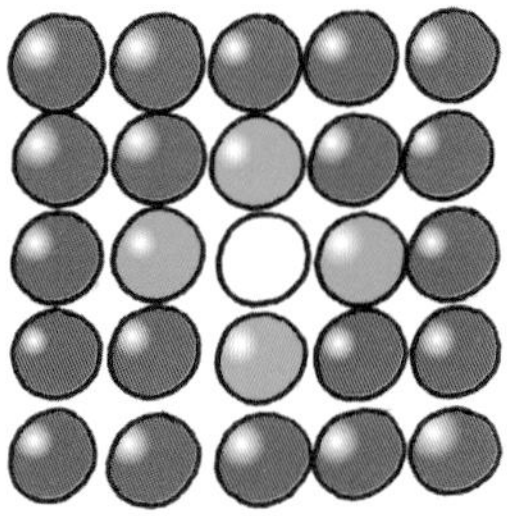

Each piece of bunting has five rows including the foundation row. When you have completed all the rows, work the needle and thread back through the beads so that the needle is in the correct position to add the next daisy chain section.

At the end of your length of bunting make a loop of 24 seed beads. Follow our chart above to add the pattern.

For a different effect, try alternating the bead colours or make the square a solid colour as in the bunting on the right

Make short lengths of bunting to hang between two branches of your tree, or a long length to wrap around the tree

Diamond bunting

How to make diamond-shaped bunting

Just like the Square bunting on page 22, diamond bunting uses simple square stitch, but this time you bring the needle out through the opposite corner so the squares lie like diamonds.

This design works well in a single colour too, and if you can't get hold of glass beads, you can use a row of coloured seed beads. As before, make short lengths to hang between branches of your tree, or a long length to wrap around the tree.

Shopping list

4 packs of size 11° seed beads:

- 1 silver lined (SL) bronze
- 1 silver lined (SL) green
- 1 silver lined (SL) blue
- 1 silver lined (SL) violet

Faceted glass beads, red, green and blue

Beading needle, size 10

Beading thread, size D, black

1 First make a hanging loop of 25 seed beads of your choice, then pick up a glass bead and five SL violet seed beads. Work back along the row of seed beads, adding pairs of beads to lie next to the first row, just as you did for the square bunting on page 22. Work four rows and then work your needle back through the beads to the other end of the last row.

2 Pick up a glass bead, then change to another colour of seed bead to make the next diamond. Keep adding beads and diamonds, changing colour as you go. Make the bunting as long as you like and finish off with another loop of 25 beads.

You can change the effect of diamond bunting by playing with the colours you use. Have fun!

Design your own decorations

How to use our blank charts

Photocopy and enlarge these brick stitch and square stitch blank charts to create your own Christmas decoration designs. They can be as large or as small as you like and you can use as many or few colours of beads as you wish.

The square stitch chart is made up of 20 beads deep and 20 wide, while the brick stitch diamond chart goes from two beads to 20 in the centre row, and back to two at the bottom. Use half this chart to make a triangle.

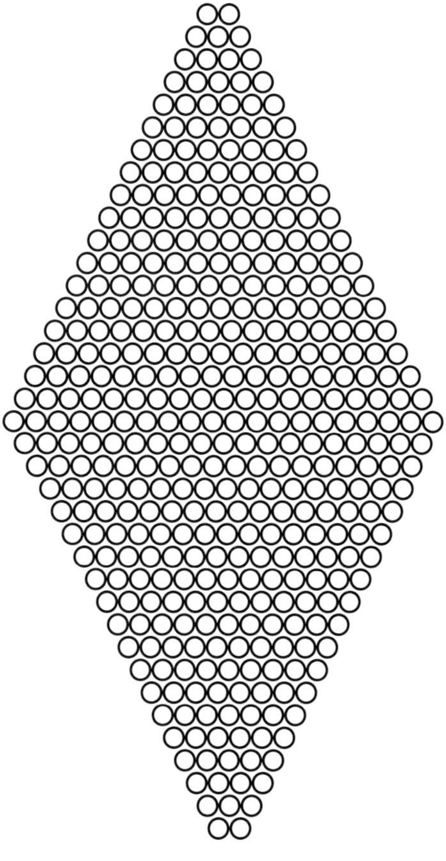

Other booklets in this series: Daisy Chains • Beaded Mandalas • Earrings • Beading on a Loom • Peyote Designs

Mail order

If you would like to join our mailing list, find out more about the next booklets, beading kits and worksheets in the series, or order more copies of our booklets and bead packs, please fill in the form below:

item	quantity	total £
● **CHRISTMAS DECORATIONS BOOKLET** **£6.99** Plus 75p p&p each		
● **DIAMOND DROPS BEAD PACK** **£6** Plus 75p p&p each		
● **BEADED MANDALAS BOOKLET** **£6.99** Plus 75p p&p each		
● **OTTOMAN BRACELET BEAD PACK** **£6** Plus 75p p&p each		
● **DAISY CHAINS BOOKLET** **£6.99** Plus 75p p&p each		
● **DAISY CHAINS BEAD PACK** **£6** Plus 75p p&p each		
	grand total £	

Name: ______________________

Address: ______________________

____

____

____

____

Postcode: ______________________

Tel no: ______________________

PAYMENT AND CONTACT DETAILS
Please make cheques or postal orders payable to:
The Useful Booklet Company Ltd.
Post this form, or a photocopy, to:
The Useful Booklet Co. Ltd.,
PO Box 3294, Stratton-on-the-Fosse,
Radstock BA3 4WL.
enquiries@usefulbooklet.com,
www.usefulbooklet.com
For overseas orders, please write or email for details of postage and payment.

● Please add my name to your mailing list (please tick box) ☐